The Philippines

The Philippines is an archipelago consisting of some 7,107 islands. With the Pacific Ocean on its eastern seaboard and the China Sea to the west it has a coastline twice as long as that of the United States.

The land consists of narrow, fertile plains and mountainous interiors, with Mount Apo, the highest in the country, rising to 3,000 m (9,690 ft). The climate is tropical, with temperatures rarely falling below 21° C (70° F).

There are about 52 million people living in the Philippines which makes it the seventeenth largest country in the world in terms of population. Filipinos are a multiracial mix of Malay, Chinese and Spanish descent.

Agriculture is the most important export industry, with coconut oil, fruit and vegetables, sugar and timber predominating. The manufacturing sector is, however, growing more rapidly.

In *We live in the Philippines*, a cross-section of people tell you what their life is like – life in the mountains and on the plains, life in the big cities and life in the isolated rural areas. The author, Gilda Cordero Fernando, is a writer and managing director of GCF Books, a publishing company in Quezon City in the Philippines.

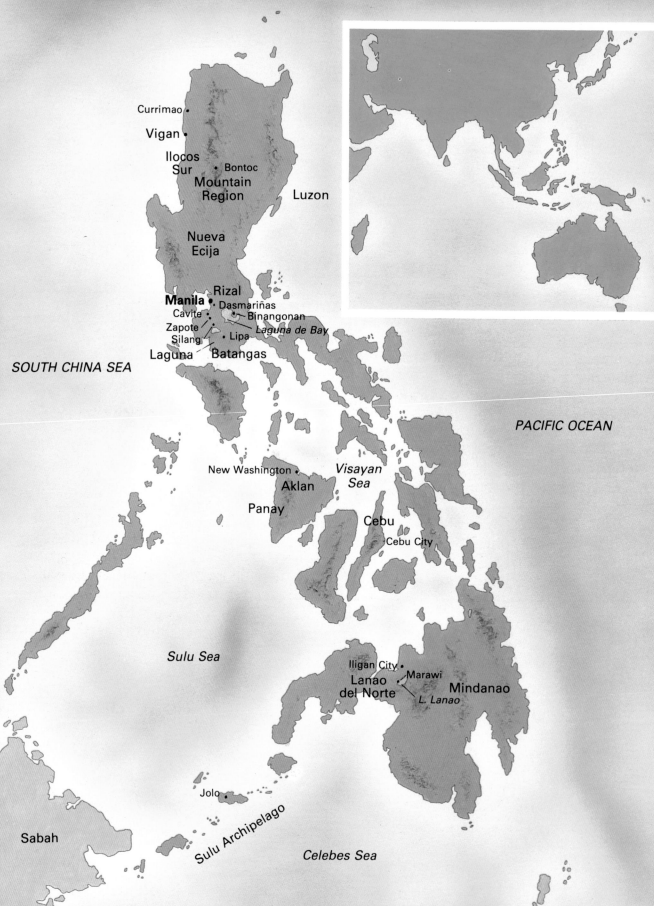

Batanes Province

Currimao

Vigan

Ilocos
Sur

Bontoc

Mountain
Region

Luzon

Nueva
Ecija

Rizal

Manila

Dasmariñas

Cavite

Binangonan

Zapote

Silang

Lipa

Laguna de Bay

Laguna

Batangas

SOUTH CHINA SEA

New Washington

*Visayan
Sea*

Aklan

Panay

Cebu

Cebu City

PACIFIC OCEAN

Sulu Sea

Iligan City

Marawi

Lanao
del Norte

L. Lanao

Mindanao

Jolo

Sabah

Sulu Archipelago

Celebes Sea

we live in the PHILIPPINES

Gilda Cordero Fernando

The Bookwright Press
New York · 1986

Living Here

We live in Argentina
We live in Australia
We live in Brazil
We live in Britain
We live in Canada
We live in the Caribbean
We live in Chile
We live in China
We live in Denmark
We live in East Germany
We live in France
We live in Greece
We live in Hong Kong
We live in India
We live in Indonesia
We live in Ireland
We live in Israel

We live in Italy
We live in Japan
We live in Kenya
We live in Malaysia and Singapore
We live in Mexico
We live in the Netherlands
We live in New Zealand
We live in Pakistan
We live in the Philippines
We live in Poland
We live in South Africa
We live in Spain
We live in Sweden
We live in the Asian U.S.S.R.
We live in the European U.S.S.R.
We live in West Germany

Further titles are in preparation

First published in the United States in 1986 by
The Bookwright Press
387 Park Avenue South
New York, NY 10016

First published in 1985 by
Wayland (Publishers) Ltd
61 Western Road, Hove
East Sussex BN3 1JD, England

© Copyright 1985 Wayland (Publishers) Ltd

ISBN 0–531–18024–7
Library of Congress Catalog Card Number: 85–71718

Phototypeset by Kalligraphics Ltd
Redhill, Surrey
Printed by G. Canale & C.S.p.A., Turin, Italy

Contents

"The customers are attracted by the decorations"

Romeo Dejar is 23 years old and a jeepney driver, operating on the Zapote-Silang route south of Manila. His vehicle, a converted U.S. Army jeep, cost him 40,000 pesos (over $2,000) even without the decorations.

When the U.S. Army brought the Willys jeep over to the Philippines in 1945 they can have had no idea what Filipinos would make out of it. We extended the back part to accommodate fourteen to eighteen passengers; then we started to work on the paintwork and decoration.

Now there are 27,000 jeepneys in Manila alone, not counting the *"colorum"* or unregistered ones. The jeepney is the fastest, cheapest and most popular means of transport all over the Philippine Islands. Sturdy, economical and easy to maintain, these workhorses can plow through dust, mud, deep ruts, rains, typhoons and sizzling heat.

Curtains, usually crocheted by the driver's wife, are hung across the windows of the vehicle. The external decorations may include two or twelve nickel plated horses; there may be two or twenty radio antennas (but not necessarily a radio). The best jeepneys, of course, do have radios as well as stereophonic tape decks which play all the latest pop tunes. Usually the jeepney has its name on the roof – *Road Master*, or *King of the Road*, in a plastic crown with a pair of wings.

Romeo collects the fares from the passengers in his jeepney.

I used to be involved in the buying and selling of coffee. That was how I was able to earn enough to buy a jeepney. Without decorations it cost me 40,000 pesos ($22,000). The decorations cost up to 22 pesos ($1.20) each but jeepneys have to have them. Customers are attracted to the best-decorated jeepneys.

Although I own the jeepney, I rent it out to two other drivers and we alternate on different days. They give me a fixed amount and everything they earn above that is theirs. On a good day, a jeepney driver can earn a hundred pesos ($5.50). Jeepney driving is better than other jobs

Jeepneys are a common sight in towns and cities all over the Philippines.

that only pay a minimum wage of 1,500-pesos (about $82) a month.

Since there are never enough buses, the jeepneys are always popular. Passengers have to grab a seat and hang on for dear life because we do not wait around.

In the rural areas jeepneys carry more than just people. They are loaded up with sacks of rice and corn, tall tins of biscuits, baskets of fish and vegetables, children, chickens, sometimes a live horse and occasionally a coffin!

"Coconut farming is the lazy man's occupation"

Mang Tirso Caradang is 60 and a coconut farmer in the province of Laguna. He owns a small plantation of about 100 trees which together yield about 1,000 coconuts a month.

Ninety percent of all people in this province earn at least part of their living from coconut farming. It's often called the lazy man's occupation because coconut farmers spend most of their time sitting around waiting for the nuts to ripen. My 100 trees produce about 1,000 coconuts a month. These I sell either as whole nuts for eating, as dessicated coconut which is used in cooking, or as copra.

Copra is the dried kernel of the coconut. It is extracted from the outer shell, or husk, and then dried. Because it is so warm here in the Philippines, we can let the kernels

Mang Tirso Caradang with his carabao (water buffalo) which he uses to transport his coconuts to market.

dry out in the sun. The copra can then be processed to yield coconut oil. Coconut oil is an essential ingredient in some soaps, and shampoos, detergents, edible oils, margarines, vegetable shortenings, synthetic rubber, glycerin and hydraulic brake fluid. One thousand mature coconuts yield about 226 kg (500 lb) of copra from which about 114 liters (25 gallons) of coconut oil is obtained. Copra is produced throughout the tropics, but the Philippines is one of the world's leading exporters.

Coconut palm trees grow best near to the sea on low-lying ground where there is plenty of water. Tall ones grow up to 30 m (100 ft) or more. Palms are propagated from the unhusked, ripe nuts. These are simply laid on their sides in nursery beds and covered nearly all over with soil. The seedlings can be planted out in four to ten months. The palm will start bearing

Coconut palms grow up to 30 m (100 ft) in height.

fruit in about five years and can go on yielding profitably for about another forty-five years or so.

I am lucky because I actually own my plantation. Many farmers in the Philippines are tenant farmers. A tenant coconut farmer is only allowed to keep about twenty percent of his yield. The rest goes to his landlord.

Besides money from my coconuts, I derive some additional income from the fruit trees I plant. These yield bananas, papayas, guavas and cacao (from which chocolate is derived). I also cultivate a variety of beans and yams, and keep 120 white leghorn chickens. With my small concrete house, one son working in Manila making false teeth, and my other son a radio announcer I am a happy and fulfilled man.

"Muslim girls have three kinds of education"

Putli, her sister Indah and their brother Ahmad, live in a remote area near Jolo City in Sulu. This is a strongly Muslim area where children know little about life in the Christian north of the country.

There are something like 3,000 islands in the Sulu Archipelago and the island of Jolo is one of the largest. Our main town of Jolo is the capital of the province of Sulu and about 40,000 people live there. This is quite a dangerous place to live because there is always fighting going on between government soldiers and Muslim rebels. People around here do not like being controlled by a government that is so far away.

Putli, Indah and Ahmad practice reading the Muslim holy book – the Koran.

There are no real schoolbuildings here. Our classes are held in the house of someone called the *barangay* leader (a *barangay* is a bit like a local council). This is just an ordinary house with flimsy partitions to divide it into classrooms. Older children go to school in Jolo itself. It's too far to walk there so they usually stay with relatives or friends in the city.

The southern part of the Philippines, including the Sulu Archipelago is a Muslim area. Most of the rest of the country is Christian. Here, Muslim girls have three kinds of education.

The first kind is the same as that given to children in other parts of the country. This is called *matrasa*. We learn to read and write and how to count, add and subtract. It's hard to get good teachers in Jolo. The one who teaches me is only a high school graduate. There is one teacher here who has a university degree, but she lives in another area. She arrives late on the first and only bus on Monday and goes home early in the afternoon on Friday.

At the beginning of a new school year the classes are always quite full. But the number of children coming always drops because children have to help their parents to run their farms. They have to husk coconuts, feed the cows, fetch water from the well and look after younger brothers and sisters. I have to do these jobs as well, but I always try to find the time to go to school. Many of the children at school come from a long way away and have to walk four or five kilometers (up to three miles) just to get here. When the typhoons come, they cannot get in at all.

As well as *matrasa*, we also have *elmo akirat*. This means learning about Islam. We go to a house of one of the elders for an hour each day and learn to read the thirty chapters of the Muslim holy book

Putli's brother Ahmad sharpens a knife on the verandah of the family home.

– the Koran. Our parents pay the Koran teacher in the form of rice or money. She knows the Koran by heart and can easily spot our mistakes. When we get something wrong, she pinches us!

The third kind of education that girls receive is traditional in this area. It teaches us how to find a good husband. We are given a prayer bath, where we hold seven kinds of sweet flowers, two eggs, a candle and perfume. This gives us charm and beauty. We also believe that there are other ways of making a man love you and stay with you. But those are our secrets.

"We fishermen are very superstitious"

Nelson Cawaling is 31 and a fisherman from the province of Aklan on the island of Panay. He lives in New Washington, a busy port some 10 km (6 mi) from the provincial capital, Kalibo.

Aklan, where I live, is the northernmost province of the island of Panay. Most of the people in this province live by fishing or farming. My boat is called a *banca*. It has a streamlined hull, an old marine engine and two floats to keep it stable in the water. I usually fish about 8 km (5 mi) offshore, using multiple fishing lines to catch small tuna. On a good day I can earn as much as 200 pesos (about $11). On a bad day I am lucky to make thirty pesos. I could earn a lot more if I could take ice with me and stay out longer, but there is no ice plant here. Once I have brought the fish to shore I give them to my wife. She either takes them to market or sells them right on the beach.

We fishermen are very superstitious. We know how important it is to know the moods of the sea. We accept that there are *engkantos* (the "enchanted ones or mermaids") who rule the sea and to whom all fishermen must pay respects by performing certain rituals and sacrifices. When my *banca* was new, I was told to kill a chicken and smear the hull with its blood. My father-in-law, who owns two boats, made sure that we used the best chicken blood, although we could have got by just using fish blood. Pigs' blood is best, but

Nelson prepares his line for another day's fishing.

we didn't have a pig.

Pigs' and chickens' blood is supposed to ensure that we get a good harvest, for just as pigs and chickens pick at anything along their way, so boats smeared with their blood can pick up any fish that are swimming in their path. In other parts of the Philippines, cooked food, like rice cakes or chickens, are placed on bamboo rafts and set afloat towards the intended fishing ground.

Some fishermen say that they can hear the *engkantos* when they are out at sea. They sound like neighing horses, crowing cockerels, chirping birds, croaking frogs, singing or guitar strumming. I have never heard them and I'm not sure that I ever

Nelson's banca *has two floats to keep it stable when the sea is rough.*

want to either. To protect ourselves we wear amulets, which we call *anting-anting*. These may be made from coconut palms blessed on Palm Sunday or strands of the wig, or bits of clothing from an image of the dead Christ.

The Filipinos are great fish eaters. The average Filipino eats about twenty-nine kilos (63 lb) of fish a year. This is twice the world average. Throughout the Philippines are scattered 600,000 fishermen with their families dependent upon their catches for sustenance. I am proud to be one of them.

"We have no running water in our house"

Luz Gamilla is 29 and a pocket maker at a clothing factory in Dasmariñas, a town in Cavite Province. Dasmariñas is a government relocation center for squatters uprooted from the city of Manila.

I am one of 1,000 workers here at the Dasmariñas Garments Corporation. Ninety percent of the labor force is women. The factory provides the labor for the manufacture of ladies' summer and winter coats and jackets. All materials for the garments are supplied by our wholesalers in Europe including buttons, buckles and other accessories. We produce 30,000 winter coats from April to September and 40,000 summer coats from October to March. They are distributed in West Germany, Belgium, the Netherlands, France and Great Britain.

This is a big factory, with fifteen production rows. Each one has preparation tables for pattern making and cutting. The cutting is done with a machine that can slice through fifty layers of cloth at once. Then the cut sections are sewn together by us women on sewing machines that are all programmed for a particular operation. I am a pocket maker, which is quite a skilled operation.

The government has fixed a minimum wage for all manual workers. I earn just over six pesos an hour, or nearly fifty pesos (about $2.75) for an eight-hour day. Wages are low in this industry because

Luz at work behind her sewing machine at the Dasmariñas Garments Corporation.

14

there is stiff competition from Thailand, South Korea and Sri Lanka. There is usually plenty of overtime, though, when we earn another 1.15 pesos above the normal rate. Even so, there is never enough to live on. Between us my husband, who is a day laborer in construction, and I earn about ninety pesos ($5) a day. From this we spend about thirteen pesos on rice and twenty pesos on meat daily. I have to shop every day because we can't afford to stock anything. Another fifteen pesos goes on other daily needs like laundry, sugar, lard, salt, vinegar and matches. We usually go without breakfast and just drink a cup of rice coffee with sugar. We have no running water in our house so we have to buy it at a private tap nearby and carry it home in buckets.

The Corporation employs about 1,000 people who make garments for the export market.

We pay ninety pesos a month in rent and twelve pesos ($.66) for electricity, although all our cooking is done on a wood stove. We gather the firewood ourselves when we're not too tired. Otherwise we buy it. Transportation is the biggest problem. It costs us twenty-four pesos a day to get myself and my husband to work and our two children to school by jeepney. When there's no money, the children have to miss school. I can get credit from the factory, but once I've reached my limit I have to borrow from a neighborhood "loan shark" at "five to six." This means that five pesos borrowed in the morning becomes a debt of six pesos by nightfall.

Life is hard. I have this cousin who works as a chambermaid in a London hotel. She's always writing and asking me to join her. Who knows? Perhaps someday I'll raise the fare to go to England. Guess what I'll do with my first week's pay? I'll buy one of those jackets I made!

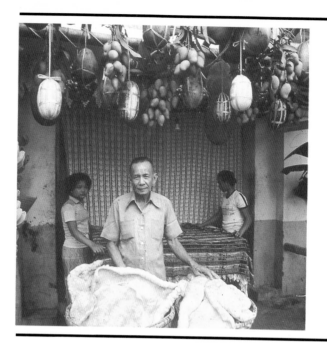

"A passion play is staged every night of Holy Week"

Narciso Benzon of Vigan, Ilocos Sur, is 74 and a retired butcher. Each Holy Week, he is the keeper of a shrine which he decorates with dried pigs' skins, fruits and vegetables.

Palm Sunday is the first day of Holy Week, probably the best-loved religious festival in the Philippines. To celebrate the triumphant entry of Christ into Jerusalem on Palm Sunday, the Filipinos braid young coconut fronds into interesting shapes to wave aloft during the Mass. The palms are decorated with flowers, grasshoppers and birds made out of leaves. In Malolos, old women lay their black veils on the ground for the priests to walk on. In neighboring towns the priest may ride a donkey through churchyards full of palm-waving devotees. The coconut palms are later attached under the windows of houses to protect the dwelling from lightning and typhoons. Ashes of blessed palms are burned underneath the trees in a plantation to ensure a good harvest.

Palm Sunday is also the day when I set up one of the fourteen shrines of the Via Crucis which are erected in different locations all over Vigan. Each shrine contains a model version of the crucifixion and is paid for and tended by the same person each year. The shrines are decorated with the fruits of the earth and other products

Narciso supervises the setting up of his shrine before the procession arrives on Palm Sunday.

that the shrine-keepers live by.

I am a retired butcher, and my sons still carry on the business. So I decorate my shrine with whole, dried pig skins, as well as farm products like garlic, coconuts, papayas, green mangoes, turnips and bananas. A religious procession passes through the city, calling at each of the shrines in turn. After the procession, I give away everything displayed to the towns-people. The next day the shrine is dismantled. I believe that participating in the Via Crucis is good for my soul, but also good for the business, which is still thriving.

From Holy Monday to Holy Wednesday there is a public reading of a holy book on the passion and death of Christ. This is done in a house or church by the old women of the community. In most little *barrios*, or villages, a *cenaculo*, or passion play is staged in groves or on river banks every night of Holy Week. These are dramas depicting scenes in Christ's life and are complete with costumes, castles and painted backdrops. Some even include things like smoke and fireworks.

On Holy Thursday and Good Friday only serious music is played on the radio. Children are not allowed to laugh or make a noise, and fish becomes very expensive in the market because people are not supposed to eat meat. Good Friday is a day for grieving and for mournful processions of dazzling, bejeweled religious statues depicting the passion and death on flower-bedecked silver floats. Good Friday is also important because it is the day when medicinal plants are gathered by witch doctors from the forest.

Easter Sunday is a joyous day when children are made to jump as high as they can, as a symbol of the risen Christ. This, it is believed, will make them grow tall.

The Palm Sunday procession passes Narciso's shrine.

17

"Gang-members are tattooed from head to foot"

Generoso Z. Llanora is 40, and a policeman and guidance counselor at the Manila City Jail. The jail is a temporary detention center in the northern sector of the city, which is notorious for its gangs.

I have been in the police force for seventeen years; the last two I have spent in the city jail. I started out as a traffic cop; later I became a detective. Here in Manila, a policeman has to play the part of a judge and a doctor; he has to deliver expectant mothers to the hospital; attend victims of stabbings; separate feuding husbands and wives; and arbitrate in squabbles between neighbors.

The city jail, to which I am now assigned, is situated in the northern sector of the city, notorious for its gang violence. Gang-members are tattooed from head to foot. From their tattoos you can find out to which gang they belong. They have names like OXO, *Bahala Na*, Commando, and Sputnik. Their gang is like a brotherhood; it offers them protection. In the slums it is difficult to exist without protectors. If a gang-member is sick, the gang gives him money. If he escapes from prison he is given aid and shelter. On the other hand, a member of one gang automatically becomes the enemy of another gang, and this is where the trouble starts.

The ancient building where I now work houses 1,600 detainees accused of all sorts of crimes. It is a temporary detention center where suspects are held before their cases are heard.

Policeman and guidance counselor Llanora preaches to the inmates of the Manila City Jail.

Once a person has spent any time in prison it is very difficult for him or her to go back to a normal life. Outside the prison, no one is interested in taking care of ex-convicts. As a Christian, I see my work here as teaching the inmates not to lose hope. I give regular *cursillo* classes. *Cursillo* means a "little course" of spiritual lectures. Some prisoners become loyal followers. My assistant rectors came originally from different city gangs: one was a murderer, the other a thief, and the third a rapist.

Since I introduced the *cursillo*, there has been a marked improvement in the inmates' behavior. So far, there have been no riots or escapes, and the assaults on prison staff or other inmates have all but stopped.

Outside of my work, I like to interest myself in the lives of the families of the people in prison. I deliver letters to the relatives of those prisoners who have had no visits. I personally deliver letters to people as far away as Taytay, Tanay, Calamba and Cabuyao.

The pay of a policeman in Manila is not high. I live in a shanty with my wife Elsa, who is a music teacher. My two sons work abroad, one as a computer technician in Jeddah and the other as a bookkeeper in California. I live a humble life, but my efforts have not gone unrecognized. I was recently given a humanitarian award by a civic club, so I feel that I am well blessed.

Many of the inmates of the jail sport tattoos. These indicate which gang they belong to.

"I have a cure for everything"

Helen Quicho is 42. She has been selling medicinal herbs in the shadow of the church in the Quiapo district of Manila for fourteen years. She opens her stall at the same time that the church opens its doors.

I am one of about 100 medicinal herb vendors who operate in the area by Quiapo Church. The market stalls here sell most things that anyone could want, at very low prices. People can buy rice cakes, brassieres, parrots, almanacs, watches, mourning veils, kung fu shoes, make-up, paper flowers, sliced pineapples, dressed chickens, knives, kettles, army jackets, video tapes, fake dollars and feather dusters. Anything you care to name you can be sure Quiapo has it.

Different streets specialize in different things. For shoes, you go to Carriedo Street. Ronquillo Street is the place for sports equipment, while musical instruments, radios and tape recorders are sold, amid a deafening noise, in Puyat Street. Cloth and groceries are to be found in Carlos Palanca Street.

My supply of herbs is delivered daily by a jeep that comes down from Montalban, a nearby wooded mountain area. I pay the supplier weekly and on brisk days, he only has to wait by my stall for a short time before I can pay him his due. I earn a minimum of twenty to twenty-five pesos ($1.25) a day and a maximum of fifty pesos on Fridays. Friday is the busiest day because it is the day of the Black Nazarene, the patron of Quiapo. The Black Nazarene is a statue of Christ bearing the cross which was brought from Mexico in the seventeenth century. Thousands of people come from all around to attend the devotions, hear Mass, light candles, walk on their knees and kiss the feet of the image of Christ. Once they have finished inside the church they step outside and are swallowed up in the bustle of commerce.

My customers are mainly those people who cannot afford to buy bottled drugs from a druggist. For a few cents they can buy some medicinal leaves, flowers, buds, succulents, seeds or roots, oils or powders. I also sell instructions on how to make them into decoctions, infusions, liniments, vinegars, poultices, ointments, washes and baths.

I stock more than one hundred different

Anything and everything can be bought at the market in the Quiapo district of Manila.

kinds of herbs and I have a cure for just about everything – high blood pressure, worms, malaria, dog bites, snake bites, despondency, rheumatism, gallstones, nose bleeds, pimples, deafness, nervousness, lice, carbuncles, dizzy spells, ulcers and even cruel mothers-in-law, bad luck and body odor! There are baths for the newborn and its mother, rock crystals for diagnosing witchcraft, beaten bark to make into shampoo and cactus for use as a hair conditioner. There aren't many customers who leave my stall unsatisfied.

Helen waits for customers by her medicinal herb stand.

"In Bontoc the only occupation is farming"

Bughong Pepe is a highland farmer from Bontoc, a mountainous temperate region in the tropical northern part of the Philippines. It is an area thick with pine trees, ferns and wild orchids, waterfalls and streams winding in deep gorges.

From his home in the sky, long ago, Lumawig, the God of the Bontocs, descended upon our lands. He had decided to live on earth and go in search of a wife. He journeyed all over the mountain region but could not find the woman he was looking for. Then, in Bontoc, he found two industrious sisters in a garden gathering beans. Lumawig picked one bean of each variety, tossed them into the baskets and instantly the baskets were filled. He married the younger of the sisters.

Lumawig could take a small chicken, feed it a few grains and it would be fully grown. He could fill a basket with rice just by putting in a few kernels. We believe that it was Lumawig who taught our ancestors how to plant seed, how to nurture the young plants, and how to reap.

That is why in Bontoc the only occupation is farming. That is why we have, with our bare hands, terraced the mountainsides to plant rice, producing what many people hail as an engineering marvel. Religion forms an important part of our agricultural life. There are rituals to ensure good rice harvests, rituals to allay

The rice terraces of the mountain region have been described as the eighth wonder of the world.

22

Mock fighting is a feature of many celebrations, or cañaos, *in the Bontoc.*

storms, and rituals to drive away cold and the fog. There is a rain dance and a rite for driving out birds and rats. There is a ritual for planting sweet potatoes and a ritual to make black beans grow. There are harvest rituals and storing rituals.

Rice is so important in the life of the people here that the eight periods of the primitive Bontoc calendar correspond to agricultural activities. The pitched roof of a Bontoc house serves as a granary and stores enough rice for use until the next harvest. If you are rich and have a lot of grain to store your roof is high; it is lower if your income is middling; it is flat if you are poor. My roof has a medium incline.

Filipinos tend to overspend for a fiesta and the Bontoc is no exception. Our celebration, called a *cañao*, is three days of continuous eating, drinking, singing, gong music, dancing and mock fights. The whole village and the neighboring ones are fed. *Cañaos* are held for weddings, wakes, peace pacts, and other important occasions. It takes years to prepare for one.

My eldest daughter is an old maid but Por-en, born twenty years later, is now 14. So I have started to store food for a *cañao* in case she weds, which I hope she will. I am stocking up on preserved pork and *carabao* meat. The long strips of meat are stored in big heirloom jars. Each jar may contain a whole cut up pig costing 4,000 pesos ($220). A good *cañao* could require five to twelve of these jars. Heavy salting and the cold weather keep the meat fresh.

Cañaos also call for *tapuy*, Bontoc's traditional rice wine. Glutinous brown rice is boiled and made to ferment with a homemade yeast till it produces a strong abundant juice. In a wedding the bride's father drinks the most *tapuy* – after all he is losing his daughter and has spent his lifetime savings on her.

23

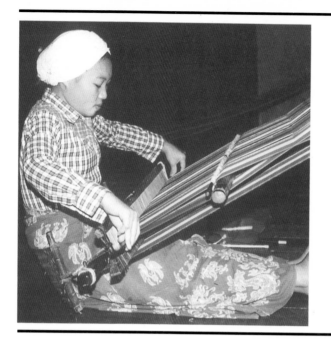

"I was betrothed at 7"

Babae Paoti is 29 and a weaver. She makes _malongs_, the principal item of Muslim dress among the Maranaws of Marawi. Marawi lies in Mindanao province on the north shores of Lake Lanao, some 760 m (2500 ft) above sea level.

The _malong_ is a cloth tube worn as a long skirt and tucked snugly around the waist. It is worn by both males and females below a long, tight-sleeved blouse with a closed neck and brass buttons for the lady, or a shirt with narrow sleeves for the man. For ceremonial occasions, such as a dance performance, the lady's _malong_ is slung over one shoulder.

Competition to the handwoven _malong_ has come to Mindanao in the form of cheap, imported Chinese cotton garments, western blue jeans and T-shirts and the pajama, which many men now seem to prefer to the _malong_.

I spend my days at my backstrap loom weaving _malongs_ in the dim light and poor ventilation under my house. The floor space of the house is too small to accommodate the bulky weaving machinery. Handweaving is a dying art nowadays. The old master weavers have died. Their sons work abroad in well-paid jobs and are able to send their weaving mothers enough money to take up less back-breaking work. Weaving skills are no longer valued and weaving techniques are

Babae at work on her loom beneath her house in Marawi.

Many of the houses of the Marawi weavers are beautifully decorated.

neither handed down by families nor taught in schools.

Like many Muslim women in this area I only stayed at school for three years. I was betrothed at 7 to my husband Dumadalug (which means "thundering"), who was 10. Our parents arranged the marriage among themselves and when I turned 14, I and Dumadalug began to live together. Now we have four sons and a happy marriage.

The colors of the clothes that people wear all have special significance here in Mindanao. Yellow and maroon can be worn only by royalty. White is the color of mourning, while black is a symbol of dignity. Black clothes are worn by men on formal occasions.

Green is the color of peace and of the Islamic religion. Red is worn by everyone and has no special significance. Someone who returns from a pilgrimage to Mecca, the holiest of Islamic shrines, becomes a *Hadji-a* and is allowed to wear a white turban. I am a *Hadji-a* and this is why my turban is white. A successful pilgrim is welcomed with red flags planted all over his yard (or yellow flags if he is royalty). A red flag is also placed on the roof of a house after a murder has been committed. This signifies that a feud is brewing between two families or tribes. A red flag can also signify that a child has been born. (The flag is yellow if the child is a member of royalty.) A green flag indicates the birth of a girl; a white flag means a stillbirth.

In the old days, these flags, and other things besides, were woven by Muslim girls in the traditional way. Now, we weavers have enough work on our hands just weaving *malongs*.

"Typhoons stronger than instruments can measure"

Pipay Guisando is 40 and a housewife in Batanes, a clutch of little islands on the northernmost tip of the Philippines archipelago. She can tell in her bones when a storm is coming.

The dry season in the Philippines is from December to May and the wet season is from June to November. The hottest temperature (in May) averages 28° C (83° F) while the coldest temperature (in January) is 25.5° C (78° F). August, September and October bring the treacherous, circular-moving typhoons spawned in the Pacific.

Batanes, where I live, bears the brunt of the typhoon's first fury but the islands have adjusted to the situation. The trees here are shorter and more gnarled; the staple foods of the people are root crops, like yams and sweet potatoes. Neither the bamboo clumps nor the easily blown nipa huts on stilts that characterize the rest of Luzon are found in Batanes. The houses here are tiny, whitewashed fortresses that hug the earth.

Since typhoons in Batanes are sometimes stronger than instruments can measure, the walls of my house are made of stone and lime at least three-quarters of a meter (2½ ft) thick. Even little one-room houses have thick walls that make them look much bigger than they really are. The roof has a grass thatch about a meter (3¼ ft) thick. During strong typhoons, my husband, Edong, and I throw a rope net over the roof to stop it from blowing off. In the town, a reserve of special grass, called *cogon*, is grown communally by the inhabitants for the repair and maintenance of all the roofs.

People here on Batanes like to tell strangers tall stories of *carabaos* being blown away during a typhoon. Actually, we're so used to typhoons that if a 120-kph (75-mph) storm passes over we consider it "normal." Farmers continue plowing their fields as if nothing were happening. During a 150-kph (93-mph) typhoon, the farmer will finally squint up at the leaden sky and admit that maybe there's a storm.

The *barrio* where I live is 20 km (12 mi) from Basco, the capital of Batanes. However, we are separated by a channel and therefore never receive storm signals. Around here, we mostly rely on folk wisdom to foretell typhoons. If the afternoon

sky briefly turns a canary yellow, a strong storm is coming. If the yellow persists for ten to twenty minutes there will be a storm but not a strong one. If some migratory birds that normally do not appear during a certain season are seen a storm is sure to follow in a week.

Certain diseases like asthma and rheumatism are sensitive to humidity and air pressure. Some people have learned to associate discomfort in their knees, hips and back with specific kinds of weather. When I feel a typhoon in my bones I tell the children to call in the masseur. Then I stock the larder with yams and make sure the *carabao* is safely home.

Some children from Batanes enjoy a ride on a carabao.

"10,000 to 11,000 ounces of gold a month"

Peter Bading is 52 and a foreman in the Antamok gold mines in the mountain region of Luzon. He is also a respected elder of the Kalinga tribe and his wife still sports the traditional tattoos.

Although the Spaniards were already searching for gold in the sixteenth century, the warlike inhabitants of this region made sure that they never found it. In fact, organized mining did not really begin here

Peter walking through the maze of tunnels that make up the Antanok mines.

until 1903 during the early part of our term of American rule. Originally, the Benguet Corporation, which operates the Antamok mines, was run by Americans.

I have now been with the company for thirty years and five months. I started out as a mucker and have gradually worked my way up to foreman. The hierarchy in the mines works something like this: the foreman gets to scold the "boss," who scolds the *capataz*, who scolds the miner, who scolds the mucker. The mucker is at the bottom of the pyramid, he fetches the tools and drills for the miner. Together, miner and mucker do the man-sized job of blasting the mountain, gouging it out, propping up the roof of the mine with beams, making the tunnels, drilling and hauling out the debris. The *capataz* is a supervisor from the junior staff, either a new graduate or someone promoted from the ranks. As foreman, I am a senior staff manager responsible for about 200 people. I translate underground what was planned by the engineers above the ground.

It is so hot 500 m (1,600 ft) underground that the miners wear as few clothes as possible.

Once extracted and roughly broken by the miner, the ore is further broken down in a ball mill (a revolving cylinder full of fist-size metal balls). Then it is passed through screens which filter out the gold dust. This is put into tubs and subjected to heating at enormous temperatures, which liquifies and purifies it. One thousand eight hundred people work all these operations in two shifts. For supervising the extraction of about 7,000 tons of ore a month, I am paid a basic salary, plus a production profit and bonuses. I think I am well paid. I have been able to extend my house, buy some rice terraces and get a car and a refrigerator.

The economics of mining gold has changed over the last fifty years or so. In the thirties, rich veins jutted out from the hillsides. A mining company simply had to follow a streak to get a bonanza. The gold was near the surface and easy to mine. Now all that has changed. The surface mine has gone and we have to dig tunnels down to 500 m (1,600 ft) to strike gold. We work on new mines, but we are also reworking what has been mined before. The price of gold has risen from its level of $35 an ounce before the Second World War to $400 an ounce. So mines that were once thought uneconomical can now be worked again. Perhaps the low-grade ore that we are putting back into the ground will become good gold again for our grandchildren.

The Benguet Corporation produces 10,000 to 11,000 ounces (283–312 kg) of gold a month. It sells everything to the Central Bank, which is the treasury of the Philippines, at the official gold price quoted daily in the London Metal Exchange. In the interests of safety, the gold extracted from Antamok is only partially refined; it still contains iron and copper impurities. The Central Bank has it further refined into almost pure gold before it becomes part of the country's gold reserves.

"The catches are sold to the highest bidder"

Higinio Bunuan is 33 and a fish fry catcher in Currimao, Ilocos Sur, which has a long and fertile coastline. He and his brother-in-law Porfirio catch the little fish in nets as fine as mosquito netting.

The tasty white-fleshed milkfish, or *bangus*, is the most popular dish on the Philippine table. It is a silvery, salt water fish with many spines which has been successfully reared in captivity for many, many years. Some people say that the pond cultivation of fish was introduced to these

Higinio shows a trader his latest catch.

islands by the Chinese, but I don't know whether this is true.

Although the milkfish can be reared in ponds, for some reason the females have never been able to spawn in captivity. Perhaps it is because of the temperature of the water, or the depth, or the current; no one can say for sure.

The females, about a meter (3.28 ft) long,

lay their eggs in the deep sea. The young are then caught by the current and brought to the shore, where people like me can fish for them. The richest spawning grounds of the *bangus* fry are to be found along the coastlines of Batangas, Mindoro, Ilocos, Cebu, Romblon, Bicol and the Davao Gulf.

Once we have caught the fry in our fine nets we empty them into plastic basins to count them. They are very difficult to count because they are transparent. All you can see is their eyes.

Because all the fry are caught in territorial waters, the municipal government handles all the bidding for them. The fish fry markets in this area are located in Dampalit, Malabon, and in Hagonoy. The bidding is carried on between wholesale buyers who act as representatives of the main buyers. These are located in big towns and cities like Manila. The bids are made before the fry are caught and a price and quota are fixed. Then the catches of all the fry gatherers are sold to the wholesale buyer who bid the highest price. The fry are delivered to the buyer's house when the quota is fulfilled – 1,000 from this fisherman; 2,000 from another and so on. In the buyer's house the fry are stored in clay pots which keep the water cool. The pots are covered so that the fry think it is always night time. They are fed on egg yolk or fine flour for about five or six days. They then turn a slightly darker color and are ready to be flown to the main buyer who pays between thirteen and twenty pesos (10¢ to $1) for each minute fish. He rears them in special fishponds until they weigh one kilo (2.2 lb). Then they are ready for the table.

Higinio and his brother Porfirio fish for fry on the shoreline of Currimao.

"Women plant rice to the rhythm of guitars"

Justo de la Cruz is 63 and a tenant farmer of long standing. He lives in Nueva Ecija, part of the Central Plains of Luzon and often called "the rice granary of the Philippines."

The cultivation of rice starts in June or July, when sacks of choice *palay* (unhulled rice grains) are soaked for twenty-four hours in drums of water. They usually sprout in about three days. While the seedlings are growing the farmers clean and shore up the low dikes which divide the irrigated rice fields.

In the smaller fields of Nueva Ecija, plowing is a communal, volunteer activity. All the workers ask of the farmers is that they provide a hefty lunch. After the plowing, the fields are harrowed to remove stones and weeds. Then planting can begin while the earth is newly turned and cool.

Farmers believe that the best time to plant is when the moon is bright and the sky is full of stars. Frequent lightning and thunder in May, we believe, will mean poor grain when the rice is harvested. Rains immediately before or after All Saints' Day (November 1) mean there will be a fine harvest.

Women, ranged in a row and moving backwards, plant rice to the rhythm of guitars. Planting is always a competition to see who can plant the neatest and

Workers harvest the rice on Justo's farm.

32

sturdiest row, without getting backache or collapsing before the end of the day.

In the old days before the coming of the tractor, planting was a really joyful time – a race between the men with their harrows and *carabaos*, and the women planters. The fertilizers used were all natural – dung from the *carabaos*. At harvest time, the countryside would be dotted with *mandalas*, large haystacks of drying grain stalks.

Before too many pesticides killed them off, fish could also be harvested from the rice fields. When the rains came the waters of the fields rose and overflowed the dikes, joining them to the waters of the river. Mudfish and catfish would be carried along to the fields where they lived in the mud and multiplied. A farmer's wife could easily catch enough mudfish and catfish to last three days. The mudfish season lasted until October, when the *amihan* wind began to blow and the fish would return to the river.

Although the carabao *is still used to plow the rice paddies, it is rapidly being replaced by the tractor.*

All that has changed now, of course. Chemical fertilizers are used that do not really rejuvenate the soil. Today, mechanical threshers are so efficient that threshing and harvesting can be done at the same time. The *mandalas* have all but disappeared.

With irrigation and other advancements it is no longer possible to follow the progression of the rice growing season. Water is available for irrigation all the year round. There used to be a season of colors – yellow for the dry season; green for the planting season; then one morning everything would be gold, and it was harvest time. Now, some parts of the field may be green at the same time that others are yellow or gold. I think it is a pity that we have lost this natural rhythm but I suppose it is inevitable.

33

"A college education can last eight years"

Teresa Maria Custudio is 18 and is studying for a degree in political science at the University of the Philippines in Manila. She was born in Cavite City and comes from a family of four girls and six boys.

I was born in the year Ferdinand Marcos came to power and I have never known any other president. In 1972, when I was 6, martial law was imposed. I am what the press here call a "martial law baby." Martial law officially ended nine years later but few Filipinos really believe that it has been abolished. Although elections were held in 1984, no one really had any faith in the results. Many martial law babies are awakening to the rights they have missed and are actively protesting against the dictatorship.

The system of education here in the Philippines has always been subject to the influence of the people who conquered us. From the Spaniards, who arrived in 1521 and left in 1898, we learned only one "R" – religion. Schools were simply catechism classes run by the priests on Sundays. When the Spanish regime ended, only a very small percentage of the population could read and write.

When the Americans took over the Philippines in 1898, they offered free elementary education to everyone. Religion was no longer made a compulsory subject, and English became the new medium of instruction. Subjects taught were reading, writing and arithmetic, geography, literature, civics (which later became social science and history), health and physical education.

There is no doubt that the education given to us by the Americans was good

Teresa with some of her friends at the University of the Philippines.

education, which taught us the importance of such things as truthfulness and cleanliness. But everything was presented from the American viewpoint. Philippine history told us that we were always rebels, not heroes; while our national anthem took the tune of the American song *Maryland, My Maryland*.

I suppose it took us four years of cruel Japanese redirection to make us realize that we were really orientals. Since the end of World War II our system of education, while still being patterned on the American system, has tended, in the last decade or so, to look more towards the east for inspiration.

Education in the seventies took a more practical turn. There was less Shakespeare in the curriculum, and more vocational subjects, like agriculture, management, science and technology, were introduced to try to teach Filipinos the skills needed to find jobs.

There is no shortage of colleges and universities in the Philippines. In fact, there are over 1,000 colleges, 63 state universities and 37 private universities. But most of them are located in Manila and other big cities. Some new agricultural colleges have been built in the rural areas but there are still not enough to stop the movement of students from the villages into the cities.

Agriculture, of course, remains the backbone of the Philippine economy. The center for agricultural education and research is the University of the Philippines College of Agriculture in Los Banos, Laguna Province. Near the college is the International Rice Research Institute, which offers programs for rice farmers and rice technologists from all over South-east Asia.

The University of the Philippines, where I am studying, is one of the best universities in the country. The campus occupies 400 hectares (990 acres) and is said to be the largest in the world. It was founded in 1909 and moved to its present site here in Quezon City in 1948. Students come here at age 17 and usually stay until they are 21 or 22, but a college education can last up to eight years. My course is not as long as that and I am looking forward to going into the outside world to put what I have learned into practice and try to turn our country into a real democracy.

The arts and sciences building of the University of the Philippines.

"I have been served two arrest warrants"

Sister Christine Tan is a nun, working in a squatter colony in Leveriza, Manila. She is a radical who marches in protest rallies and comforts those on picket lines and in political detention centers.

What do you do if one of your nuns arrives at your door carrying a rolled mat with a rifle hidden inside it entrusted to her by a neighbor because he would be killed if caught with it? What do you do if you are sought for sincere advice by a group of peasants who want to kill an evil *barangay* leader? What do you do if one of your

community leaders comes home one evening inside a plastic bag?

The first two incidents are common occurrences in the nuns' houses in the rebel areas of Mindanao. The last happened in our vicinity. In Agusan, a communist guerilla who had been shot by the military crawled to the sisters' house. They put him on the kitchen table, washed him, and called a doctor to remove the bullets. Were they justified in helping him or were they giving "aid and comfort to the enemy?" Our superiors, our Bishop, even the Jesuits have nothing to advise us along that line. We sisters just have to confer among ourselves and with those assigned to the rebel areas. Then we reflect deeply on what God really wants us to do.

I live here in Leveriza, by choice, in a makeshift house with five other nuns. Most people live in boxes, with ceilings so low that the inhabitants cannot stand

Sister Christine at work among the poor at the squatter colony in Leveriza.

The Philippines is a strongly Catholic country and the churches are often richly decorated.

up. The main occupations for the squatters are washing clothes, selling lottery tickets and boiled ducks' eggs and pasting together paper bags made from old telephone directories for market stallholders at seven pesos (38 cents) for 1,000 bags.

There are no definite mealtimes in Leveriza because often there are no meals. Yet we have taught the people here how to share. The squatters make little towels which they sell. But they know the proceeds are not just for themselves. They voluntarily seek out the neediest people and buy rice for them.

I think that you have to hear the perpetual coughing of the people here and smell the open sewers to know what being poor really means. Only then can you presume to know the people's needs. I see the Good Shepherd not just as the benign figure cuddling an innocent lamb. I see him too punishing the greedy and the dishonest with the crook of his staff.

Many of the nuns in the Philippines who work among the poor are, like me, very radical in their beliefs. I have been served two arrest warrants (both of which were later rescinded) and was one of the first to write to the president when martial law was imposed. Like many other people, I also opposed the recent elections because I felt that we could not trust the results. We liberal nuns teach the poor to fight for their rights. They cannot be victims forever or society will never change.

"Boiled rice is eaten with everything"

Maria Dacanay owns and runs a native fast-food restaurant in the city of Lipa in Batangas. The meals she serves range from fish cooked in banana leaves to boiled pig's head.

Highway restaurants like mine depend for their business on the hunger pangs of travelers. They are usually situated on halfway points of long trips between provinces. In my restaurant, which is called "Dacanay's" after me, I serve about thirty or forty different types of dishes. We cater to all sorts here. There are planters who come in colorful skirts and *bandanas*, and businessmen with their families who arrive in Mercedes Benzs.

In all restaurants where fast service is important the method of serving customers is called *turo-turo*. This literally means "point-point." An array of dishes and soups is placed on the counter and the customer points to the one he wants. These are then ladled out on to plates and brought to the customer's table by a waitress. This is why my restaurant is also called a *turo-turo*.

I'm up at about 5 o'clock every morning and soon off to the market to buy fresh food which I load on to a jeepney. On Mondays, my shopping list includes a live pig which we butcher ourselves. Our customers insist that their food be fresh. If the crabs are not nipping the cook's fingers or the fish thrashing in the basket, they'll go somewhere else.

Except in big city restaurants vegetables

In Maria's restaurant the customers simply point to the dish they want.

are never made into raw salads. They are usually boiled with fish or pork, or sautéed with garlic and onions. Favorite vegetables are eggplant, squash, swamp cabbage *(or kangkong)* bittermelons *(or ampalaya)* kidney beans and sweet potatoes. People who reach the age of 100 will always tell you that their strong bones and good eyesight are due to these vegetables.

The Philippines are surrounded by water so fish is always plentiful. If you are rich you eat big fresh fish, if you are poor you eat small fish, salted and dried. Fresh fish is cooked simply – broiled and oozing with fat on the live coals, cooked in a broth with ginger, or cooked in a broth soured with green tamarinds. Fish may also be wrapped in banana leaves and boiled in vinegar till dry.

Beef is not as popular with Filipinos as pork or chicken. *Carabao* meat (from the work animal) is also eaten. In my *turo-turo* people come for the meat dishes because meat is associated by Filipinos with festivities, with something special. Vegetables and fish are more everyday foods.

Boiled pig's head is usually sliced and marinated in vinegar with onions and spices. The pork can be made into *adobo*, a spicy dish which could probably qualify as our national dish. The ribs are charcoal broiled. The intestines and blood are made into a delicious pitch black stew. The skin is made into a glorious crunchy crackling which is dipped in vinegar with pepper.

Chicken is often fried; beef is boiled with potatoes, cabbage and a sausage. There are many more types of cooking but these are the most popular.

For dessert you have a choice of fruit in season – mangoes, pineapples, bananas, papayas or watermelons. They may be served fresh, preserved in syrup, or made into puddings, pies and candies.

Turo-turo *restaurants are a common sight on highways throughout the Philippines.*

"People prefer mass produced plastic images"

Francisco de la Victoria is a carver of religious images, or *santos*. He lives in Cebu City on the island of Cebu, where the first Catholic Mass in the Philippines was believed to have been held.

Cebu City is famous for Magellan's Cross, which was erected by the great navigator in April 1521.

The carving of *santos* is a tradition that began soon after the Spaniards came in 1521. Magellan was searching for spices, landed in the nearly spiceless Philippines and was killed by a fearless Cebu chieftain. As with all their Catholic conquests, Spain was interested in the number of souls they could baptize. So the Philippines was not only a political conquest but a religious one as well.

Conversion of the natives to Christianity created an immediate demand for churches, altars and *santos*. In the early days of colonization very little religious art came into the country. The early sculptors worked from prints of saints, book decorations and religious pamphlets to produce carvings that are now in museums and collections all over the world. To endow their *santos* with life-like qualities the carvers sometimes used unconventional materials like *carabao* cheese.

The Spaniards were extremely cruel masters but they did bring western art and culture to the Philippines. Our beautiful churches with their exquisite carved *santos* are living proof of this.

Catholicism has always been the religion of the majority in this country. The favorite saints depicted in religious statues are: San Miguel trouncing the devil; San Pedro with his cockerel; San Roque with a wound on his knee and his dog carrying a loaf of bread in its mouth; Santo Niño of Cebu; and San Isidro Labrador, the farmer-saint whose angel friend plowed his fields. Then, of course there are the different versions of Christ and the blessed Virgin Mary after whom so many Philippine girls are named.

The Philippines is blessed with a great variety of trees, many of which are used to provide timber. As a sculptor I use hard, medium or soft wood depending on whether I want the statue to last or whether I want to make it quickly and cheaply. Some Philippine hardwood is so heavy that a less than life-size statue can hardly be lifted by twelve men. There are also woods that are unburnable. Heavy wood is generally made into the large formal statues for churches. These have ivory faces, bodies made to look like ivory, wigs, eyes of painted glass and velvet robes.

Medium and soft woods I make into smaller statues used for home veneration or decoration. These are all wood. Everything is carved from the curls on the *santo's* head down to its toes. I am one of the last practitioners of the dying art of *santos* carving. Either devotions have gone out of fashion or people prefer ugly, mass produced and cheaper plaster and plastic images.

"I charge whatever people can afford"

Ignacio Blancada is 72 and a *hilot*, or healer living in the lakeside town of Angono. He cures sprains, dislocated bones and muscle pains through massage. He has been a *hilot* since he was 15.

Here in the rural areas of the Philippines sick people are mostly treated by unschooled healers like me. Our bright young doctors would rather practice medicine in Manila or in the U.S.A.

Two spinster aunts taught me the art of massaging for healing purposes when I

was 15. My wife, Luring, and I have now been *hilots* for many years. I take care of the male patients while my wife looks after the women.

All sorts of cases come my way – last week I had to go to Santa Cruz (several towns away) to attend to a child who had fallen from a table and injured her arm and leg. Another time I stayed a whole month in Romblon (an island in the south) to attend to the school principal's left arm. He had trouble straightening it out because he had damaged his elbow. I massaged his arm everyday with coconut oil and prayed over it. With the grace of the Lord before I left he could bend his arm freely. I don't have fixed fees. I charge whatever people can afford – one peso (5 cents), or even less, some vegetables or a pack of cigarettes. It is not an easy life but I am respected and well loved by the townspeople.

Ignacio and Luring mix herbs outside their home.

Ignacio treats a small child who has complained of pains in the chest.

Each *hilot* has his own way of detecting an injured bone or muscle. One who treats only children uses a special kind of mirror. He runs the surface of this small mirror over the bare body of the child – the breastbone, the ribs, the waist, the back. If the mirror sticks to a certain spot the trouble is there. The *hilot* then dips his fingers in coconut oil and massages the part, making the sign of the cross over it. The massage is repeated three times a day, before sunset.

Another *hilot* may use fresh banana leaves for detection. A leaf is first wilted over a fire and drenched with coconut oil. It is then placed on the front of the body and then at the back. If the leaf sticks to any part of the breast or back then that is the trouble spot. The *hilot* concentrates on massaging there.

A third way used by some *hilots* to detect and cure broken bones is the use of splints and a medicinal mixture. The latter is usually pounded ginger. This is applied to the injured part. Two bamboo splints are tied up with rags to brace the fractured bone. Sometimes *areca* nut peel is also used to cushion the splints and keep them in place. Over the afflicted part the *hilot* says secret prayers believed to have strong curing powers.

As well as *hilots* or masseurs like us, there are other medicine men (or women) of the poor. They are the *arbularyo*, who use medicinal herbs, the midwife who delivers babies, and the diviner who detects illnesses caused by spirits.

At first the government used to laugh at us, calling us all quack doctors. But now they have learned our value to the community, they send medical doctors over to help us improve our techniques and make them more scientific.

"I earn less than a waitress at McDonald's"

Priscilla Andaya is a Grade I teacher at the Binangonan Elementary School in Rizal Province. She teaches children of 6 and 7 English, Pilipino, math, civics and culture and character building.

I suppose that like all public (or state) school teachers in the Philippines, I am overworked and underpaid. After a long course of education leading to an elementary school certificate (ETC) or a bachelor of science in education (BSE) the salary of the average teacher is about 700 to 800 pesos ($38 to $44) a month. This means that I probably earn less than a waitress at a McDonald's hamburger restaurant!

There are three levels of education here in the Philippines. There are elementary (or primary) schools, of which some are funded by the state and are free and others are funded privately. They are for children

Priscilla points out the letters of the alphabet to the class at Binangonan Elementary School.

age 6–13 years. The private schools always give a better standard of education. From 13–17 some children (a much smaller number) go to the mostly private secondary schools. Then there are the universities and colleges that take students over 17 years of age. The school year here starts in June and ends in March with the vacation falling at the hottest time of the year.

Although elementary schools like mine are funded by the state, there is never enough to go around. Year after year I face the problems of lack of facilities. There is usually a shortage of text books and desks, sometimes no classrooms and always no chalk.

A public school teacher has to do more than just teach. I cook noodle soup for sale to the children at ten centavos a bowl during lunch break; I am responsible for the vegetable plot at the back of the school (which is also used for the pupils' benefit); I promote fund-raising events; I serve as

These children seem to be enjoying their time at school.

a clerk in the district education office; I sometimes have to take care of the clinic and even the lavatories.

Outside of school hours I help organize and conduct adult education classes, make home visits, take censuses and surveys, participate in flood damage surveys, work for the district Red Cross, and am active in fund raising for the church, in reforestation and conservation, as well as one hundred and one other things too.

With all this work, I suppose you must be wondering why I haven't dropped dead. Believe it or not, I actually enjoy my work. I am a respected member of the community and that means a lot to me. Come rain or shine, in spite of long hours and meatless meals you will always find me in front of my blackboard, unless, that is, I am attending to some flood control project, of course!

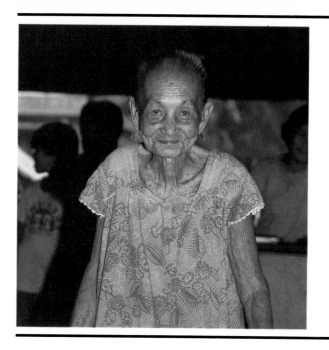

"Pinipig making is a dying art"

Nana Rosita is 80 and a *pinipig* maker in Batangas. She thinks that in today's world of instant food and artificial flavorings, the taste of real cooking has gone.

Pinipig is a breakfast cereal, a little like Rice Krispies (only ten times more delicious!). Here in the Philippines we eat it in a cup full of hot drinking chocolate. *Pinipig* can also be made into all kinds of tasty rice cakes.

The manufacture of *pinipig* is quite a backyard industry here in Batangas. I've been making it for almost as long as I can remember. First the newly harvested young grains of unhulled rice are toasted in a clay pot over a wood fire. Then my partner and I winnow the toasted grains to remove the chaff. We do that by tossing them into the air from large, flat baskets. The grain is then placed into a crude, tinsided machine which has rollers to flatten them out into thin flakes which is *pinipig*.

I am sad to say that *pinipig* making is a dying art these days because people would rather eat fast than eat well. People just can't be bothered to take the trouble to make *pinipig*. City people would rather have an instant pancake with powdered coffee. When I was young, a woman's time was spent cooking and housekeeping and food tasted like food. No one used a pressure cooker, a *mechado* stew simply had to be simmered for hours until the sauce became thick and oily and the fatty juices oozed out.

In those days you couldn't just saunter over to the supermarket to buy a piece of

Nana winnowing the toasted grains of rice to remove the chaff.

Pinipig *making is a disappearing art as fast food becomes more popular.*

pork and a tub of ice cream for Sunday lunch. You had to raise and butcher the pig yourself. Our ice cream was cranked up for hours in a wooden bucket full of cracked ice and no one would dream of adding starch to hasten the freezing. Instant foods were not yet invented and monosodium glutamate, the savior of many doubtful cooks, did not exist.

Today even fish is flavorless because there are so many pollutants in our rivers. In the old days you simply boiled vegetables and shrimp sauce together and it was delicious. Now you cook your kidney beans with a whole large fish, onions, tomatoes and lots of monosodium glutamate and still it is tasteless!

There are probably too many people in the world today. Food has to be diluted and extended to make it go around. Hordes of people eat relentlessly every day so the growth of chickens and pigs has to be speeded up. It used to take six months to rear a decent chicken and nine months before a pig could be butchered. Now you can have a "miracle chicken" weighing one kilo (over 2 lbs) in forty days, while pigs are puffed up with chemical feeds.

It's not only *pinipig* that is disappearing. So are many of our fruits. Even *carabao* milk is getting scarce because *carabaos* are being replaced by tractors. Well, tractors may be more efficient, but you can't milk them!

47

"A Christian city in a Muslim area"

Camilo Cabili is 50 and for twenty-five years has been the mayor of Iligan City, the capital of Lanao del Norte, and the most highly industrialized city in the Philippines.

Until the Americans arrived in the Philippines, Mindanao, the southern part of the country, and Luzon and Visayas in the north were almost totally isolated from one another. The north was under Spanish rule and entirely Christian. Mindanao remained independent and Muslim. But as the north became more modern and developed, so Mindanao became backward. In the twenties and thirties, the Americans tried to reverse this trend. Entire landless populations were moved from Luzon and Visayas to create Christian communities in the south. This led to bitterness which became a struggle for land and political power. The struggle goes on to this day between Muslim guerillas and government forces from the north.

Mindanao produces something like fifty percent of all the corn and coconuts in the Philippines, twenty percent of all the rice, fifty percent of the fish, forty percent of the cattle, almost one hundred percent of all the bananas sold for export, eighty-nine percent of the nickel and cobalt, ninety percent of the iron ore and sixty-two percent of the limestone.

Iligan City is a Christian city in a predominantly Muslim area. It is also the most highly industrialized city in the Philippines. The manufacturing industries located here include steel, cement, rubber, paper, flour, coconut oil, copra, charcoal, fertilizer, bricks and chemicals. These industries have made the city truly progressive and polluted. It is something of a land of milk and honey for job seekers, specialists and inventors. The per capita income of the workers is higher than the national average. Salaries here are the highest outside Metro (Greater) Manila. Even teachers and clerks enjoy comfortable lives. Residents of less progressive Muslim towns all around come to Iligan to see the latest movies, to shop and to get their supplies of medicine.

Some people say that this city is ugly, but I love it. Iligan is the bay, the hills and the smoke stacks. Iligan is also the waterfalls – a dozen of them – including the

Muslim mosques are common throughout the southern part of the Philippines.

mighty Maria Cristina, which is 30 meters (100 ft) higher than the Niagara Falls and one of the major waterfalls of the world. The Maria Cristina hydroelectric plant generates enough electricity to light Iligan, Cagayan de Oro, Marawi and Pagadian. When fully harnessed its 950-megawatt capacity can illuminate the whole of Mindanao.

Camilo likes to dress up and take part in all the festivals in Iligan.

"Ninety percent of our movies are imported"

Eduardo L.A. Pachta is 23 and works in one of the twenty outlets of "Burger Machine." He says his customers prefer his hamburgers to those produced by the American companies because they taste Filipino.

Sandwiches and hamburgers were introduced into this country by the Americans during the colonial era, although it is only in the last two or three years that Filipinos have begun to treat a hamburger sandwich as lunch. Before then they were just considered snacks. But with westernization and progress came hurrying. Servants who could cook a fussy sit-down meal were no longer available and the hamburger came into its own.

Although it tries its best to look American, "Burger Machine" is wholly Filipino-owned. We have survived the onslaught of the multinational chains like McDonald's, with their sophisticated sales techniques, imported placemats, plastic cups and free rides simply because our customers prefer our hamburgers. They say they taste more Filipino – spicy and juicy, with lots of onions, eggs and pepper. They like them better than the U.S. hamburgers that rely mostly on the taste of the meat. People go to U.S.-franchised places mainly because of the atmosphere. They like to feel they are "in the States."

"Burger Machine" hamburgers are about the cheapest on the market. That's because we have a small overhead. All our

Eduardo's "Burger Machine" van operates in the lot of a gas station.

50

hamburgers are served from vans so there's no need to pay high rentals on restaurants. Most of our vans are located in gas stations so the owners don't need to build lavatories and washrooms. The van is not really a van at all. It has no engine. But it does contain everything I need – a steamer, grills, a refrigerator, a soft drink dispenser and a cracked ice holder. Twice a day the hamburger patties, buns and coleslaw are delivered. If the location proves to be unprofitable they just put the van on to a trailer and resettle it somewhere else in the city.

Of course, there is a ready market for fast food here in Metro Manila. It is an enormous metropolis with a population of 7 million – nearly one-seventh of the country's total. It covers the massive area of 636 sq km (245 sq mi) and is made up of four chartered cities – Manila, Quezon, Caloocan and Pasay – and thirteen municipalities. And it's growing all the time both inland and on the seaward side on reclaimed land.

The hamburger is not the only American influence here in the Philippines. They introduced our political system and our system of education. They brought Christmas trees, blonde-haired dolls and Christmas carols. Ninety percent of the things we read and the movies we watch are imported.

The enormous city of Metro Manila offers a ready market for fast-food chains like "Burger Machine."

"The houses of the rich were huge"

Martin I. Tinio is the curator of Casa Manila, a recreation of a rich man's house of the nineteenth century. It is one of three old houses located in Intramuros, the old walled city within Manila, which is now being reconstructed into a museum of Philippine life.

In the nineteenth century, during the days of Spanish rule, town life in the Philippines centerd around the church and the royal building, which stood on a plaza

Martin in one of the magnificent rooms of Casa Manila.

complex. The rich people built their houses around these centers of power. The most fashionable address of the time was Calle Real, or King's Road, which was the main street of the town.

The houses of the rich were huge. So big in fact that the servants sometimes had

to cycle between the *sala* (or receiving room) and the kitchen. The ground floor walls were up to 3 m (10 ft) thick to withstand the strong earthquakes. They were made of adobe bonded with lime, sand and sometimes egg whites and honey. The upper story, however, was made of wood. The rich man's house had very wide floorboards, sometimes 76 cm (30 in) across and 15 m (50 ft) in length. It had a tall roof of red tiles which kept the house cool. Fresh breezes wafted in and out of large windows that often measured 80 cm (31 in) high and 5.5 m (18 ft) wide. The panels covering the windows were made of wooden frameworks fitted with panes made out of the flat translucent shells of edible shellfish.

The front doors would open on to an *ante-sala* where all guests were welcomed. The double doors to the *sala*, however, were opened only to guests of high social standing or on festive occasions. The *sala* was furnished with Chinese mirrors, large framed pictures and suites of furniture.

The *sala* led to the dining area. A rich man's dining table, with the addition of two half-moon leaves at each end, could seat two dozen people. Because people liked to talk, luncheon often lasted two to three hours, sometimes spilling over to *merienda* (tea) time.

A passageway led to the kitchen, which was usually a separate unit. Cooking was done on a row of clay wood stoves in which a fire was kept burning during the whole day. Off the kitchen was an *azotea*, an open service area where meat and fish were dried and clothes were hung on lines.

The bedrooms were small and few. They invariably contained an intricately carved four-poster bed surrounded by a lace valance and had a washstand and basin nearby. In each room there would be an altar on top of which would stand carved ivory saints protected by glass domes. The ceilings of the bedrooms were painted as were the ceilings of the *sala* and the dining room.

Intramuros is the old Spanish fortified town. As well as ancient houses, it also contains the church of San Agustin, the oldest church in the Philippines, and Fort Santiago, once the headquarters of the colonial authorities. Until recently, much of Intramuros lay in ruins, but we are now trying to restore the old city and turn it into a living museum of life in the Philippines in days gone by.

One of the entrances to Fort Santiago in Intramuros.

53

"Typhoons are our worst enemy"

Mario D. Camacho is 48 and the president of the Manila Electric Company (Meralco). His office is on the thirteenth floor of a plush building. He is the boss of some 5,000 employees.

This company is one of the few remaining privately-owned distributors of electricity. Most of them are now cooperatives. It is also one of the largest corporations in the Philippines. Our main business is to distribute electricity. This means that we buy the electricity from the generating company, the National Power Corporation, and transmit it to the consumer at 220 volts within a certain, franchised area. We service the core area, Metro Manila, and beyond that to Malolos in the north, Lucena to the east, Cavite to the west and Calamba to the south. Our work is to see that our 1,300,000 customers get electricity day in and day out and that the consumption is recorded and billed.

That is not always an easy job. A bird can easily trip a transformer and cause a blackout. But typhoons are the worst enemy of our transmission system. The lines and poles are exposed to the elements and strong winds and rain combined can easily fell trees, which in turn can bring down the power lines. In 1971, the force of one typhoon twisted and snapped the tall steel poles carrying 115,000-volt wires. We had to take all the poles

Meralco's service fleet with the tall Meralco Building in the background.

down and have them redesigned and strengthened.

Here in the Philippines the pricing of electricity is what we call "socialized." This makes it different from most other countries. Households pay a different rate depending on the amount of electricity they use, measured in kilowatt/hours (KWH). Of all the households we serve, sixty percent consume 200 KWH a month or less and pay a lower rate per KWH than the other forty percent. To use 200 KWH a household probably has six or seven light bulbs, one refrigerator, one electric iron, one television set and one electric fan. For this the household would pay about forty-five pesos ($2.45) a month.

As a homeowner moves up in life an air-conditioner may be installed in the master bedroom. This will push consumption up to 500 KWH and the rate per KWH will increase accordingly. Affluent homes, with a heated swimming pool, complete

The Philippines has a high level of volcanic activity which Mario hopes will one day be converted into electricity.

air-conditioning system and lots of appliances may pay a bill of around 4,500 pesos monthly. But these people make up only about one percent of the population of Metro Manila. Most people use far less electricity than consumers in other countries. The average Filipino uses about 200 KWH a month, while the average American consumer uses around 500 to 600 KWH a month.

Of course many parts of this country, and particularly the rural areas, have no electricity supply at all. This is in spite of the enormous power supply potential that we have here. Numerous dams have been built on suitable rivers. Some of these, on the Angat, the Agno and the Magat, supply hydroelectric power stations. The high level of volcanic activity on the archipelago means that there are geo-thermal resources to be exploited; oil has been discovered, with fairly large reserves anticipated on Palawan; and a nuclear power station has been built on Bataan, near Manila. It is hoped that electricity will soon be available to every town and *barrio* in the Philippines.

"The most popular sport in the Philippines"

Manuel "Nene" Santos is 20 and an amateur basketball player for the Plaza Boys team in the Paco district of Manila. He explains why, in spite of their height and build, the Filipinos are enthusiastic basketball players.

Basketball is probably the most popular of all sports in the Philippines. In just about every town plaza you will find a town hall, a church and a basketball court. This surprises many outsiders because the Filipinos as a race have neither the build nor the height to play this tall player's game. Its popularity can probably be traced to the speed and excitement that each game brings. Also, and perhaps more important, the Filipino love for the game may be due to the ease with which they can make a basketball court.

The ring of the basket can be made from the top of an old tin can. Old planks of wood or a billboard can be used to make a backboard. In the provinces, a coconut tree becomes a goal post. A harvested field, a backyard or a quiet road can become the court. In the towns basketball goals will often be found attached to lamp posts or telegraph poles.

Basketball enjoys strong popular support. It is an exciting sport, and the fans sometimes get carried away. During a pro-fessional tournament, an unpopular call from the referee can bring a hail of corn cobs, paper cups, coins or batteries on to the court. Sensible spectators bring an umbrella to protect themselves from this barrage of rubbish.

The Filipinos take great pride in their national team. When basketball was pre-dominantly an amateur sport the team was the undisputed king of Asian basketball. However, when professional basketball became widespread some of the best amateurs were lured away from the Philippines to play in the United States and elsewhere.

Of course, basketball is not the only sport practiced here in the Philippines. Cock-fighting, for example, has been a traditional sport on Sundays and holidays for centuries. Every little township has its cockpit, called a *tupada*, to which crowds of spectators are drawn. There they place their bets on the cock which they think will win.

As well as basketball, children often like

to play *piko*. This is a kind of hopscotch, which is played in the street. *Sipa*, a game played by kicking a small ball of woven

cane, is also popular. For older and more skilled sportsmen, there is *jai-alai*. This game is a little like handball, and the game takes place in a court with two walls. Finally, we have our own martial art, called *arnis*. Each contestant holds a wooden stick and tries to get the better of his opponent by twisting movements.

Basketball has rapidly become one of the most popular sports in the Philippines. Manuel and his team practice in a local plaza.

Facts

Capital city: Manila (population 1,630,485) although the population of Metro (or Greater) Manila is nearer 7 million.

Principal languages: Pilipino (Tagalog) and English are the official languages. Pilipino, a Malay-Polynesian derivative, is spoken by 55% of the population, and English by 44%. There are more than 89 regional languages and 122 dialects; Maranao is spoken by the Muslim minority in the south.

Currency: The peso (divided into 100 centavos) is worth about 5.5 cents (May 1985).

Religion: About 85% of the population is Roman Catholic, 7% is Muslim. Minority groups of Animists, Buddhists and pagans are found mainly on Luzon.

Population: 52 million (estimated 1984). The Philippines are densely populated. There are 7,107 islands, with a total land area of 292,695 sq km (114,334 sq mi). Ethnic groups include Indians and Chinese. The Chinese minority is estimated to be over half a million.

Climate: The climate is maritime and tropical. In the north the rainy season is from June to November. In the south the rain is evenly distributed throughout the year. The temperature shows little seasonal variation. The most noticeable condition is the change in humidity. There are on average 12 typhoons annually.

Government: The Philippines became an independent Republic on July 4, 1946, and has experienced various forms of government. Martial Law (military rule) was introduced in 1972, officially ending 9 years later. The first democratic National Assembly, the Batasang Pambansa, was elected in May 1984. This Assembly has legislative power and consists of 200 members; 165 are elected. The President, as Head of State and Chief Executive, nominates the Prime Minister and 34 Executive Ministers. Members serve for 6 years, and all citizens over 18 years are eligible to vote. Local policies are governed by "citizens" assemblies called *barangays*. The Philippines is divided into 12 regional councils under the Ministry of Local Government.

Housing: An extensive government program is underway to ease the housing problem. This includes the building of town and rural housing for rent or sale to low-income families. The standard of living is below average. Wooden houses built on stilts alongside the Pacific are known as "floating villages." Such housing is common in the Philippines.

Education: There are three levels of education. Elementary education (from 6 to 13 years) is free, with schools in every *barangay* district. English and Pilipino are taught. In 1983, 8.7 million pupils received elementary education. Secondary schooling (from 13 to 17) is mainly private. In 1983, 3 million pupils received this level of education. Higher education consists of over 1,000 colleges, 63 state universities and 37 private universities. The Ministry of Education sponsors adult literacy projects and agricultural training programs. Of the population, 89% is literate, which is high.

Agriculture: Over half of the population is employed in agriculture. 35% of the land area is under cultivation. Rice is the most important crop, grown on 31% of the land, followed by maize. Sufficient rice is grown to feed the population. More then 60% of the forests are put to commercial use. Fishing is centerd around Mindanao in the south. Principal exports are coconut oil, copra and sugar. Agricultural products are now less important to the economy, the revenue falling to $121 million in 1983. Government grants encourage production of finished goods, rather than raw materials.

Industry: Manufactured goods account for 33% of the total exports of the Philippines. The electronics industry is the largest exporter; in 1983 the revenue was $684 million. Other industries are food processing, chemicals and textiles. Copper, gold and nickel are mined on Luzon. The Philippines has numerous petroleum sites around Palawan, but it is not self-sufficient. Geothermal and hydroelectric power are now being developed as part of a 5-year energy program. When complete, this energy should produce 15% of the islands' requirements. The economy is based on private investment, although government funds subsidize many industries. Tourism is a growing industry,

Glossary

aided by the tourist development plan. Over 100,000 people visit the Philippines each year.

The media: The Philippines has 15 daily newspapers, 7 in English, 6 in Pilipino and 2 in Chinese. Over 220 regional papers are published. Martial Law did impose strict press controls, but since 1981 these restrictions have relaxed. There are 5 state-owned television channels in the Maharlika network and 21 private regional channels. Forty-six of the 286 radio stations are based in Manila. The National Telecommunications Commission is the governing body of all public telecommunications.

Adobe   Sun-dried brick used for building.

Anting-anting   A magic charm, or amulet, worn as a protection against evil.

Banca   A fishing boat.

Barangay   A local governing council.

Barrio   A village.

Carabao   A water buffalo used by farmers.

Copra   Dried coconut kernels processed to yield coconut oil.

Elmo akirat   Muslim religious education.

Engkantos   "Enchanted ones," or mermaids, believed by some to live in the sea.

Fish fry   The newly-hatched young of fish, usually very tiny.

Hilot   A healer who treats patients with medicinal herbs and massage.

Jeepney   A converted U.S. jeep used to carry passengers and goods.

Malong   Muslim dress, woven in the shape of a tube, which is worn by both men and women.

Martial law   Government by the armed forces with ordinary law and civil rights suspended.

Matrasa   Elementary education.

Pinipig   A cereal made from rice.

Rebels   People fighting against established authority.

Sala   The receiving room of a house.

Santos   Religious images carved of wood or made of plaster or plastic.

Squatters   People living on land they do not own, often in crude huts.

Turo-turo   "Point-point" or fast service, as in fast-food restaurants.

Acknowledgments

All the photographs in this book were supplied by Noli Yamsuan, with the exception of the following:
Julie Dalena 48 (top); Joseph Fortin 10 (both), 11, 24 (both), 25; Meralco 54; Philippine Tourist Office 9, 22, 33, 37 (top), 40 (bottom), 45, 51, 53; Nik Ricio 26, 27 (both); Felice Santa Maria 40; Wig Tysmans 22 (top), 23, 28 (both), 29.

Index